# THE CAPE BUFFALO

## BY
## WILLIAM R. SANFORD
## CARL R. GREEN

### EDITED BY
### DR. HOWARD SCHROEDER
**Professor in Reading and Language Arts
Dept. of Elementary Education
Mankato State University**

**PRODUCED AND DESIGNED BY
BAKER STREET PRODUCTIONS**
**Mankato, MN**

# CRESTWOOD HOUSE
Mankato, Minnesota

**LIBRARY OF CONGRESS CATALOGING IN PUBLICATION DATA**
Green, Carl R.
  The Cape buffalo.

  (Wildlife, habits & habitat)
  SUMMARY: Examines the physical characteristics, behavior, life cycle, and possible future of the dangerous Cape buffalo.
  1. Cape buffalo--Juvenile literature. (1. Cape buffalo.) I. Sanford, William R. (William Reynolds). II. Schroeder, Howard. III. Title.
QL737.U53G684       1986                    599.73'58            86-32859
ISBN 0-89686-321-2

|  International Standard Book Number: | Library of Congress Catalog Card Number: |
Library Binding 0-89686-321-2           86-32859

## ILLUSTRATION CREDITS:

Cover Photo: F.S. Mitcheli/Tom Stack & Associates:
Stephen J. Krasemann/DRK Photo: 5, 17, 18, 23, 24-25, 28, 35, 38, 40-41
Jim Brandenburg/DRK Photo: 6, 27, 32
Nadine Orabona: 9, 31
Bob Williams: 10, 14
M.P. Kahl/DRK Photo: 12, 21, 45

### CRESTWOOD HOUSE

Hwy. 66 South, Box 3427
Mankato, MN 56002-3427

# TABLE OF CONTENTS

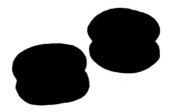

The stars blazed above the dark African plain. Grass rustled in the breeze, and a lion roared in the distance. A single campfire burned beside a muddy river.

The hunter shivered and moved in close to the fire. He had never been so close to big game animals before. "Gene, what's the most dangerous animal out there?" he asked the head guide.

Gene waited for the cry of a night bird to die away. "Well, the experts say the lion, the rhinoceros, the leopard, the elephant, and the Cape buffalo are the Big Five." He turned to the second guide. "What do you think, Alex?"

"That's not counting crocodiles, hippos, and tsetse flies," Alex chuckled. "Still, Gene's right. All five of those animals are fast, strong, and mean. None of them wants to be a trophy on anyone's wall."

The hunter wouldn't be put off. "One of them must be the champion," he said.

"I've hunted all of them," Gene said. "But the Cape buffalo is the only one that gives me nightmares. Those black monsters are big, strong, and smart. Get one of them angry at you, and *m'bogo* will go out of its way to kill you!"

"M'bogo?" the hunter echoed. "What's that?"

"That's the Swahili word for the Cape buffalo," the

*The Cape buffalo, called* m'bogo, *is big, strong, and smart.*

second guide said. "A big bull weighs over a ton. Put a bullet in his heart and he'll keep coming at you."

Gene took up the story. "The herds are peaceful enough when they're out in the bush," he said. "But just try to sneak up on them! First thing you know, they'll stampede. Imagine forty or fifty of those monsters running right at you! If you can't climb a tree, you'll have to shoot one animal and hide behind it. With luck, the herd will split and run around you."

*Many big-game hunters think the Cape buffalo is the most dangerous animal to hunt.*

"A wounded Cape buffalo is the worst," Alex added. "Most animals try to get away after they're shot, but not the buffalo. It wants revenge! An old bull will run for awhile. Then he'll circle back and wait for you in the bush. If you don't kill him when he charges, he'll rip out your stomach."

"I read a story about the Cape buffalo," the hunter said. "A buffalo chased a guide up a tree. It couldn't reach the man with its horns, so it licked him. Its tongue was so rough it tore his shoes off! Then it licked the skin right off his feet!"

"I think that's a myth," Gene said. "But I do know that a wounded buffalo will attack the next human it sees." He looked at the hunter. "Just imagine that you're the unlucky guy. If it catches you, it will stomp on you for awhile. Then it will toss you around on its horns. Two years ago, I saw a herd of buffalo throw a native guide back and forth like a beanbag."

The hunter swallowed hard. "After all that good news, what will we be hunting tomorrow?" he asked.

"I saw some buffalo tracks today," Alex said with a smile. "Why don't we go after m'bogo? If you're going to be a big game hunter, you might as well start with the best!"

# CHAPTER ONE:

A family of hoofed mammals called the *Bovidae* include some very useful animals. People drink their milk, eat their meat, hitch them to plows, and hunt them for sport. Dairy cattle belong to this family, as do water buffalo. Other important Bovidae are the yak and the American bison. But when you talk about big game animals, one Bovidae stands out—the African buffalo.

Fossils show that animals like the African buffalo have been around for thousands of years. As recently as twelve thousand years ago, stone age Africans hunted a giant buffalo named *Pelorovis*. This huge buffalo died out when the weather turned warmer after the last ice age. The African buffalo developed to fill the habitat space left by *Pelorovis*.

# A family with three subspecies

Naturalists once thought there were fifteen varieties of African buffalo *(Syncerus caffer)*. Today, they recognize only three subspecies. The best known of the three is the Cape buffalo *(Syncerus caffer caffer)*. The

Cape buffalo ranges widely, but is most often found in the open bush country of East Africa. These fierce black animals have wide, curving horns.

The second subspecies is the forest buffalo *(Syncerus caffer nanus)* of West Africa. Sometimes called dwarf buffalo, the reddish-brown forest buffalo are smaller than Cape buffalo. Their horns curve backward and upward instead of jutting out to the side. Their smaller size and backward curving horns allow them to move easily through their forest habitat.

The final subspecies is the Sudan buffalo *(Syncerus caffer brachyceros).* These medium-sized, long-legged

**The Cape buffalo is the largest African buffalo.**

buffalo are larger than the forest buffalo but smaller than the Cape buffalo. They range across the grasslands of north-central Africa below the Sahara. Sudan buffalo have reddish-brown to black coats.

# A tall, heavy animal

Cape buffalo are about the same size as the Holstein cattle found at a dairy. Adult buffalo range in height at the shoulder from forty-two to sixty-eight inches (107

*Cape buffalo are about the same size as a Holstein dairy cow.*

to 173 cm). From nose to base of tail, they measure eighty to 120 inches (203 to 305 cm). Their tails add another thirty inches (76 cm). By contrast, a large forest buffalo stands only fifty-four inches (137 cm) at the shoulder. The cows of *Syncerus caffer* are about three-fourths the size of bulls.

Full-grown bulls vary in weight. An average bull weighs 1,300 pounds (590 kg), but a large bull may reach two thousand pounds (907 kg). Old stories, however, tell of bulls that weighed as much as 2,600 pounds (1,180 kg). The smaller forest buffalo seldom weigh more than 725 pounds (330 kg).

# Watch out for those horns!

Alongside a Cape buffalo, the horns of a Spanish fighting bull look almost harmless. The buffalo's black horns are among the most dangerous in nature. Both bulls and cows have horns, but the bull's horns are longer and heavier.

From tip to tip, a bull's horns average about thirty-eight inches (90 cm). The largest pair ever taken by a hunter measured fifty-six inches (140 cm). The two horns join together at the base to form a helmet-like shield atop the buffalo's head, The shield is fully formed by the time the buffalo is eight years old. Each horn curves outward and downward from the shield before turning up in a graceful curve.

*The horns of the Cape buffalo are made of the same material as human fingernails—keratin.*

The horns are made of keratin, the same material found in fingernails. Even though the horns are hollow, they seldom break. Young buffalo have smooth horns, but grooves soon form at the base of each horn. As the animal ages, the grooves move outward.

Older buffalo often break the tips of their horns by fighting. Buffalo also wear the tips down by digging in the ground for salt. If a young buffalo chips one of its horns, the damage often forces the horn to grow at a new angle. Thus, each buffalo's horns vary in size, shape, and condition.

How strong is the Cape buffalo? One hunter reported that he saw a bull trying to rescue a wounded member of the herd. First the bull worked his horns under the dying buffalo. Then he lifted the wounded animal completely off the ground. That was a lift of more than 1,600 pounds (726 kg)!

# A grass-eater with four stomachs

Cape buffalo are grazers, just like domestic cattle. Their squared-off muzzles allow them to feed close to the ground. Like the other *Bovidae,* Cape buffalo have a horny plate at the front of their upper jaw instead of teeth. The buffalo's lower front teeth do all the cutting.

If the teeth can't cut the tough grass, a jerk of the buffalo's powerful head tears it loose.

Grass isn't easy to digest. The stomachs of Cape buffalo and other *Bovidae* have four chambers to do the work. As the buffalo grazes, the lightly chewed grass moves into the first stomach (the rumen). Digestion starts there. During rest periods, the buffalo forces balls of partly digested grass (called cud) back into its mouth. The buffalo chews the cud with its back grinding teeth.

When a buffalo reswallows its cud, the mashed-up grass passes into the second and third stomachs. Known

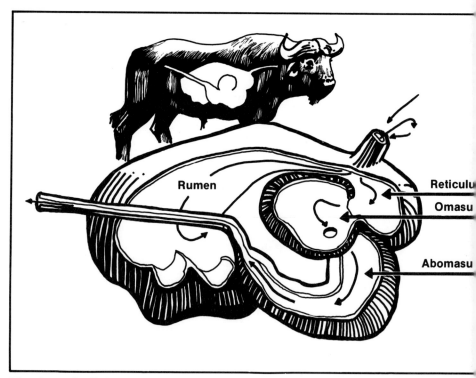

*The Cape buffalo has four parts to its stomach.*

as the reticulum and omassum, these two stomachs are mostly for storage. Final digestion takes place in the fourth stomach, the abomasum. From there, the digested mass passes into the intestines. Along with its daily intake of grass, a Cape buffalo needs plenty of water.

# A tough, brown-black hide

Cape buffalo range in color from dark brown to black. Calves are reddish-brown, with thick hair up to four inches (10 cm) long. In older buffalo, the hair grows short and bristly, except for the long, soft hair around their drooping ears. Old animals turn an ashy-grey. They often develop bald patches on their rumps.

Up close, the buffalo's tough hide smells more like that of a horse than a cow. The one-inch-thick (2.5 cm) hide protects the buffalo when it plunges through thorn bushes. Native Africans tan the hides and use the leather for shields and sandals.

# No one sneaks up on a Cape buffalo

The Cape buffalo is blessed with excellent hearing, a keen nose, and good eyes. The crack of a single breaking twig or the faintest scent of an enemy can send a herd stampeding. Hunters, therefore, must creep in downwind of a grazing herd if they want a good shot. As often as not, a sudden wind shift will carry their scent to the buffalo. That's enough to start them running. When they're protected from hunters, Cape buffalo seem to lose their fear of humans. In game parks, they allow visitors to photograph them without showing any sign of alarm.

Eyesight isn't as important to the Cape buffalo. Like dairy cattle, they can see most colors—but not red. They use their eyes to find food, and their noses and sense of taste to tell them if it's good to eat. As with many animals, they're better at seeing movement than shapes. A hunter proved this in an unusual way. Caught in the path of a stampeding herd, he pretended to be a tree. He played the part by standing perfectly still with his arms held out as ''branches.'' The panicky herd broke apart and ran by the ''tree'' without touching it.

The Cape buffalo once roamed most of Africa south of the Sahara desert. Today, the remaining buffalo have been pushed into a much smaller habitat. That's where naturalists have to go to study these dangerous wild cattle.

# CHAPTER TWO:

The Cape buffalo once roamed all of Africa south of the Sahara desert. Early explorers found large herds near the Cape of Good Hope, which gave the animal its name. Since then, hunters, disease, and increased farming have greatly narrowed the habitat. The Cape of Good Hope herds have almost disappeared.

Today, the Cape buffalo is found mostly in the grasslands that cross Africa from ocean to ocean. The herds seem to prefer open pasture. An ideal Cape buffalo habitat also has trees for cover and water for bathing

*Today, most Cape buffalo live on grasslands that have water for bathing and trees for cover.*

17

and drinking. These hardy animals have also been found at heights of ten thousand feet (3,000 m) in the 'mountains.

# A herd animal

The Cape buffalo lives and travels in herds. Naturalists believe that the buffalo find safety in numbers. Even when they're protected in a game park, the Cape buffalo stay together. In the 1800's, herds of ten thousand animals were common. Herds of a thousand or more still roam the game parks. Outside of the parks, however, the herds average only thirty to sixty animals.

*Cape buffalo almost always live in herds of at least thirty animals.*

Most herds are led by a bossy old cow. The strongest bull brings up the rear, ready to defend his herd. Because there is no single mating season, herds contain calves of all ages. The cows keep everyone away from their calves, including the young bulls. A typical herd contains buffalo of both sexes, but naturalists have found all-female and all-male herds.

Older bulls are often driven from the herd by younger, stronger bulls. At other times, they seem to leave on their own. These old bachelors sometimes form a small herd with four or five other lone bulls. They live quietly, free of the need to fight for rank in the herd. Unlike the regular herds, these old bachelors often learn to raid village cornfields. One hungry bull jumped a six-foot (1.8 m) fence to get at some ripe corn.

# A life of feeding, bathing, and resting

Each day, a Cape buffalo herd leaves its forest cover at dawn. The buffalo may walk several miles to find good grazing land. Their walking pace is only two miles (3 km) an hour. A stampeding herd, however, reaches speeds of thirty-five miles an hour (58 km)! The herds cover a small range that seldom extends more than twenty miles (32 km) from end to end. The old bachelors seem content with a range of only two or three miles (4 to 6 km).

Along with grass and herbs, the buffalo sometimes feed on the tender shoots of bushes and trees. A herd may graze in one spot for three or four days before moving on to new grass ten miles (16 km) away. If the herd senses that rain has fallen nearby, they will move there to enjoy the new grass. Water is important to the herds, and they stay near the rivers during the dry season.

The daily routine seldom changes. After grazing in the early morning, the buffalo often drift down to the river to drink their fill and to bathe. They repeat that pattern in the evening. The herd spends the rest of the day grazing and ruminating (chewing their cud while at rest). These activities take up about eighty-five percent of the buffalo's day. In hot weather, the herd moves back into the shade to escape the blistering sun.

The Cape buffalo take water baths and mud baths. A swim in the river cools them off, and helps them fight the ticks that cling to their hides. Rolling in the mud is called wallowing. When the mud dries, it helps keep biting insects away. Buffalo also will lie in the smoke from a brush fire to escape the flies. Unlike most wild animals, buffalo do not go into a panic when fire is near.

Cape buffalo don't seem to sleep for more than a few minutes at a time. They often rest standing up, or by lying down with their legs curled up under their bodies. Instead of sleeping, they seem to drowse while chewing

*The bulls are always on the lookout for danger.*

their cud. Even then, several bulls always stay alert for danger.

# The struggle for power

The young bulls fight almost constantly. Along with fighting for females, Cape buffalo battle for a higher position in the herd. Rival bulls begin by trying to bluff each other. With horns held high, they paw the ground and bellow at each other. If the bluff doesn't work, they lower their horns and charge. When two bulls meet head-on, the ground shakes with the force of the collision. Each bull pushes and shoves, trying to force his rival backwards. Finally, the loser drops to his knees or backs away.

In most cases, the bulls don't use the sharp tips of their horns in these battles. When they do gore their rival, the wound can be deep and painful. Once in a while, the bulls lock horns. As they twist and tug, one of the horns may break off. Left with only one horn, the loser cannot fight for his place in the herd.

The strongest bulls have special status. They protect the herd when danger threatens. If a lion is prowling nearby, the bulls stand between the cows and the lion. In most cases, the herd will run away rather than fight. The highest-ranking bulls also have their choice of females when it is time to mate.

# Winged partners

Several birds share the Cape buffalo's habitat. One, the white egret, often perches on the buffalo's back. The egrets eat the tsetse flies which bother the animal. This is a welcome service, for many flies stay outside the range of the buffalo's natural flyswatter—its tail. In addition, the egrets screech and fly off when the lions appear. Older, blind buffalo rely heavily on these warnings.

The red-billed oxpecker also makes itself at home on the buffalo. The oxpecker feeds on the blood-sucking ticks that cling to the animal's hide. A wallow in the mud and a visit from an oxpecker are the buffalo's tick-control system.

*An oxpecker eats insects from a Cape buffalo's nostrils.*

*White egrets help Cape buffalo by eating flies and screeching when lions come near the herd.*

# Even Cape buffalo have enemies

In areas where they've been hunted, the Cape buffalo herds move and feed by night. During the day, they hide in the forest or underbrush. Except for humans, the herds don't have many natural enemies. Lions, leopards, and hyenas will attack newborn calves. The predators must be both quick and lucky, however. Even a lion will back off when attacked by an angry cow. A two-year-old buffalo can drive off a pack of hyenas.

The herds seem to remember their enemies. If a lion has killed a member of the herd, the other buffalo will attack any lion they see. Lions have better luck with old bachelor bulls. Lacking the protection of the herd, these aging animals are killed more often than buffalo in any other age group.

Stinging tsetse flies, ticks, and other insects annoy the buffalo almost beyond endurance. The biggest danger to the herds, however, is a virus disease called rinderpest. Although they're immune to most cattle diseases, rinderpest wiped out almost ninety percent of the Cape buffalo in the 1890's. Since that low point, the buffalo have increased in numbers. They are no longer an endangered species.

*Buffalo herds are getting larger in most areas of Africa.*

# Will the Cape buffalo survive?

Left alone in a good habitat, Cape buffalo herds grow rapidly. More than eighty percent of the cows in one herd were carrying calves, and the bulls live for twenty years or more. Even so, naturalists worry about the future of the Cape buffalo. A more careful study of their life cycle may help us do a better job of protecting them.

*Cape buffalo calves are usually born during the rainy season, when there is plenty of grass for the cows to eat.*

# CHAPTER THREE:

Eastern Africa knows only two seasons—the rainy season and the dry season. Grass is scarce during the dry season, and grazing animals sometimes can't find enough to eat. If calves were born in the dry season, the cows might not have enough milk for them. That's why the Cape buffalo's calves usually are born at the height of the rainy season.

## Mating during the rainy season

On this July morning, the Cape buffalo herd is leaving its shelter in the forest. The buffalo search out the best grass, fresh and green after the heavy rains. An old bachelor bull shadows the herd, attracted by the scent of cows ready to mate. Buffalo mate the year around, but they're most active in July.

As the bull comes up, a younger bull trots out to meet him. Both animals snort and toss their heads. If the young bull could speak, he'd be saying, "Get out of here, old fellow! These females belong to me." The older bull won't back down. He bellows loudly and charges.

The ground trembles as the two bulls smash into each

other. The young bull is stronger. Step by step, he pushes the bachelor bull backward. Their hoofs dig furrows in the earth. Finally, the intruder has had enough. He slips to his knees and backs away. The young bull gores him in the neck with a lightning thrust of his horns.

The victor returns to his five-year-old cow. She has a year-old calf, but the bull pushes it out of the way. He licks the female and rests his head on her rump. At first she moves away. Finally, she stops and allows him to mate with her.

# A new calf is born!

The cow carries her calf for eleven months. A new rainy season has started. The cow beds down in the shelter of a patch of thorn bushes to give birth. Instinct tells her that the calf must be hidden until it can keep up with the herd.

The one hundred pound (45 kg) bull calf is born in the early morning. His coat is a deep reddish-brown. The cow licks him and encourages him to stand up. Four hours later, the calf is ready to follow the cow back to the herd. Still shaky on his long, thin legs, the calf totters after her. Once, when he loses sight of his mother, he bleats softly. The cow takes her calf into the herd, but she doesn't let the other buffalo come too close.

# Life is hard for a calf

The calf suckles from his mother's teats for about fifteen minutes at a time. The lush grass that the cow eats makes plenty of rich milk. The calf puts on weight quickly.

A week later, one of the watchful bulls gives an explosive warning snort. A lioness is stalking the herd! The cows and calves move behind the line of bulls. One of the older cows gives a signal. Almost at once, the herd turns and stampedes across the rolling plain. The calf cannot keep up with the running herd. Left alone, he would surely become easy prey for the lioness. But the cow stays with her calf. The lioness circles the

*A cow is a good match for any predator that wants her calf.*

watchful cow, but decides not to risk a goring from her sharp horns.

When the bull calf is old enough, he begins to graze beside his mother. At seven months, the cow's milk dries up. The calf tries to nurse, but there's no milk. Now he must live by grazing with the rest of the herd.

The days pass. The calf follows the herd to the river each day. He quickly learns to enjoy a wallow in the mudflats. Often, he's content to lie in the shade,

*Cape buffalo love a good mud bath. The mud helps keep biting insects away.*

chewing his cud. But he's also full of life. He prances and runs around in circles with his tail held straight up. The older bulls ignore him.

Just before the calf is two years old, the cow gives birth again. This time it's a female, smaller and redder than the young bull. By now, his coat has turned nearly black. His smooth horns begin to show grooves near the base. Each day, he rubs the shield at the base of his horns against a tree trunk. When the herd moves out to graze, the young bull joins the other two-year-olds.

# Surviving the dry season

The rainy season gives way to drought. The grass begins to turn brown. The water holes and wallowing spots dry up. The herd wanders across the baking earth, nibbling at the sparse grass. When that runs short, they eat twigs and small bushes. The young bull loses weight. Several of the weaker calves die.

The search for food seems endless. Driven by instinct, the herd joins with two other small herds. There's safety in numbers. A pack of hungry hyenas follow the herd, hoping for an easy meal. Vultures circle overhead.

Finally, dark clouds blacken the sky and rain falls at last. Grass sprouts almost overnight. The young bull gains back the weight he lost. He's now three years old, and weighs 1,800 pounds (816 kg). His great horns stretch almost fifty inches (127 cm) from tip to tip.

# Winning a place in the herd

In June, the large herd breaks up. Each buffalo finds its original herd by scent. The cows always stay with the herd into which they were born. But each bull must fight for his place.

At four years of age, the young bull feels strong and sure of himself. Day after day, he challenges the older males. In one losing battle he chips his horns and receives a deep gash across his ribs. Despite that defeat, he more than holds his own. Together with the other young bulls, he drives four older bulls out of the herd. They wander off to become bachelor males.

Now the young bull finds a cow that's ready to mate. He begins his courtship. As he circles the female, the herd's lookouts sound a warning. The bull wheels around, ready to defend the cow. The scent of humans and gunpowder fills his nostrils. Suddenly, a terrible pain spreads through his chest. His legs buckle under him. The herd stampedes.

The bull struggles to his feet and trots away. His chest hurts, but the bullet didn't reach his heart and he won't die. However, an instinctive desire to take revenge is driving him. He'll hide in a thorn thicket and wait. If he has a chance, he'll trample the strange animal that tried to kill him.

*A wounded bull will wait in ambush, and then charge whatever has hurt him.*

# CHAPTER FOUR:

In 1890, Cape buffalo were common all through sub-Saharan Africa. Great herds grazed wherever they found good grass and water. Naturalists believe that only zebras and hartebeests outnumbered the buffalo. Then an Italian military force brought a boatload of cattle into Ethiopia.

The cattle carried a virus disease called rinderpest. The disease swept through Africa, killing domestic cattle by the tens of thousands. But rinderpest didn't stop at the cattle ranches and village corrals. It killed many varieties of antelope and wild cattle—including the Cape buffalo. A second outbreak of the disease in 1896, left the buffalo on the edge of extinction.

# Nature thrown out of balance

Some of the antelope, such as the greater kudu, never fully recovered. The Cape buffalo did come back, but not in the same numbers. The real damage, however, lay in the effect of rinderpest on the African environment. The disease upset the balance of nature, and the damage is still felt today.

Many nomadic Africans make their living by herding cattle. When rinderpest wiped out the herds, they were left without food and money. The people moved to the cities to find food and work. A whole way of life was upset—but still the damage continued.

The grasslands, no longer grazed by cattle, became overgrown with heavy brush. Tsetse flies, the carriers of the dreaded sleeping sickness, invaded the brush. The flies kept farmers and cattle herders from moving back. In the 1930's, tractors cleared the brush and public health workers attacked the tsetse fly. Farmers returned and plowed up thousands of acres of former grassland. Many wildlife areas were lost forever.

# Cape buffalo come back

Rinderpest was wiped out in the early 1960's. Since that time, the Cape buffalo population has been increasing. Between 1961 and 1965, for example, the buffalo in Tanzania's Serengeti National Park doubled in number. Today, visitors can see herds of a thousand or more in this beautiful game park. Naturalists estimate that there are over four million Cape buffalo in Africa.

The naturalists now worry that the herds will grow too large. If they do, they may overgraze the parks and cause serious erosion. One answer is to set more land aside for wild animal parks. But Africa's human population also is growing. The people need land for their farms and villages. Little by little, they have been pushing back the edge of the wilderness.

African governments are caught in the middle. On one hand, their people need land. At the same time, the game parks bring in tourists and much-needed money. For now, the major parks seem safe. But no one knows what the future will bring,

*More and more, there is pressure to let people farm on the grasslands that Cape buffalo need to survive.*

# Poachers attack the herds

Setting up game parks doesn't end the threat to Africa's wildlife. If there is a demand for an animal's hide, horns, or head, illegal hunters called poachers invade the parks. The poachers don't care how they kill their prey. When hunting Cape buffalo, for example, they often dig pits along the buffalo trails. Then they line each pit with sharp stakes. Any buffalo that falls into the pit dies a painful death.

The poachers sell the horns to African medicine men. The medicine men use the horns for grinding "magic" powders. The poachers also export to Europe and the Americas. People with no feeling for wildlife buy Cape buffalo hoofs to use as ashtrays. They even mount the horns and display them in their dens.

After taking a buffalo's horns and hoofs, the poachers are left with up to a ton (907 kg) of tough meat. For the most part, they keep only the tongue, the kidneys, and the bone marrow. While the poachers are in the bush, they cook a little of the remaining meat into soups and stews. Their dogs eat some more, but most is left for the hyenas and vultures.

The African governments do what they can to combat poachers. The area is large, however, and the governments are poor. One useful tactic relies on air patrols. The patrols fly over the parks and spot the huts used by the poachers. Game wardens can then move in and arrest the illegal hunters.

*Luckily, hunters and naturalists are on the same side when they work to preserve habitat for the Cape buffalo.*

# What does the future hold?

A few natives have bred Cape buffalo as domestic animals. Buffalo put on weight while grazing on pasture that won't support domestic cattle. Raising buffalo on a large scale doesn't seem likely, however. Because the animals carry hoof-and-mouth disease, they can't be

shipped from one country to another. In addition, buffalo are always dangerous to their keepers.

Naturalists say, "Like all wild animals, m'bogo belongs in its native habitat." For once, big game hunters agree with the naturalists. They want the Cape buffalo around so they can go on safari and shoot them. True hunters say that bagging a Cape buffalo tests every ounce of their skill and courage.

# CHAPTER FIVE:

A hunter named Robert Ruark knows the Cape buffalo well. In "Suicide Made Easy," Ruark writes: "I am afraid of M'bogo, the big, black Cape buffalo. . . . He is just so . . . big, and ugly, and mean, and crafty. . . . And when he's mad, he wants to kill you."

The qualities that Ruark lists make the Cape buffalo a marvelous game animal. Every year hunters travel to Africa to hunt m'bogo. African governments permit the hunting, but only under strict rules. Each hunting party (called a safari) must stay within its own block of land. Each block contains thirty to sixty square miles (78 to 155 sq. km).

# An expensive sport

Hunting the Cape buffalo is an expensive sport. First, the hunters must prepare for the African bush. This means going to a doctor for shots to guard against disease. It also means buying the right clothing and the right guns. Next, the hunters must fly to Africa and travel to the jump-off point for the safari. A thirty-day safari can easily cost $10,000.00 (US).

The hunters also must buy hunting licenses. If they want to shoot a Cape buffalo, there will be extra fees.

The government collects the license fees whether or not the hunters kill their animals.

Safari guides tell hunters to carry big rifles of .400 caliber or more. They say that smaller slugs won't stop m'bogo.

# Imagine you're a buffalo hunter

A typical day on safari begins before sunrise. A servant brings you a mug of tea and a bowl of hot water for washing up. As you shiver in the cold air, it's hard to believe that the heat will be unbearable in a few hours. After breakfast, you grab your gear and climb into an open truck. The truck grinds into gear and moves off along a bumpy trail.

Sunrise brings the first heat of the day. You take off your jacket. Road dust billows around the truck when it swerves to avoid a giant anthill. Finally, the driver stops in a wooded area. Ahead is a water hole covered with green scum.

The guide leads you to a hiding place. The sounds of the bush are all around you. You hear the hum of insects, the flap of a bird's wings, and the chatter of monkeys. A herd of small deer appear, but you ignore them. You're after bigger game.

# A long wait

The hours drag by. The guide says m'bogo is nearby, but the herd is drinking somewhere else this morning. You count twenty different birds in fifteen minutes. Wildebeest and kudus come to drink. Flies swarm around your head and bite your neck.

After lunch, the guide whispers that he has an idea. You follow him along a game trail. For two hours, you claw your way through thick grass and thorn bushes. Suddenly, you see a single buffalo! It's a bachelor male, feeding in a grassy pasture. He looks black and huge and dangerous.

Slowly, on hands and knees, you crawl forward. At fifty yards (46 m), the bull looks up. "Shoot!" the guide says. "He'll be gone in another second." You bring the rifle up, but m'bogo doesn't run away. Instead, he heads right for you!

# A hard animal to kill

This bull must have been wounded once before, you think. He's lost his fear of people. Now he wants to kill you! The bull has his head up, so you aim for his heart and fire. The big .470 rifle kicks and knocks you backward. When you look up, the guide is pointing. Your shot was on target. M'bogo is down.

As you watch, the buffalo scrambles to his feet and

heads for the safety of the bush. The guide fires quickly. He doesn't want to chase a wounded buffalo. Angry to the last, m'bogo may circle back and set up an ambush.

The guide's accurate shot breaks the buffalo's spine. M'bogo goes down a second time. The guide walks over and prods the bull with his rifle. "Your shot killed him," he says. "He just didn't know he was dead."

After your bath that night, you sit by the campfire. You have a fine trophy to take home, but you're a little shaky. You can still see m'bogo's sharp horns and angry eyes as he charged toward you. "That bull really wanted to kill me," you think.

*Today, it's mostly money from hunting licenses that pays to maintain the game parks that the Cape buffalo needs to survive in the future.*

# MAP:

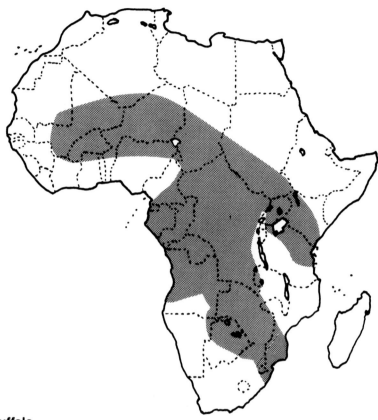

Cape buffalo
are found in
the shaded areas
of Africa.

# INDEX/GLOSSARY:

**WILDLIFE**
*HABITS & HABITAT*

**READ AND ENJOY THE SERIES:**

If you would like to know more about all kinds of wildlife, you should take a look at the other books in this series.

You'll find books on bald eagles and other birds. Books on alligators and other reptiles. There are books about deer and other big-game animals. And there are books about sharks and other creatures that live in the ocean.

In all of the books you will learn that life in the wild is not easy. But you will also learn what people can do to help wildlife survive. So read on!